# Smithsonian

# HOW TO DRAW
# AMAZING
# AIRPLANES AND
# SPACECRAFT

WRITTEN BY KRISTEN McCURRY

ILLUSTRATED BY MAT EDWARDS

CAPSTONE PRESS
a capstone imprint

# TABLE OF CONTENTS

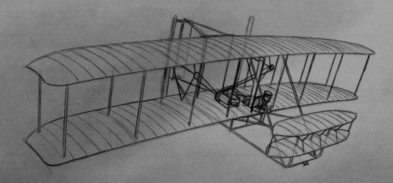

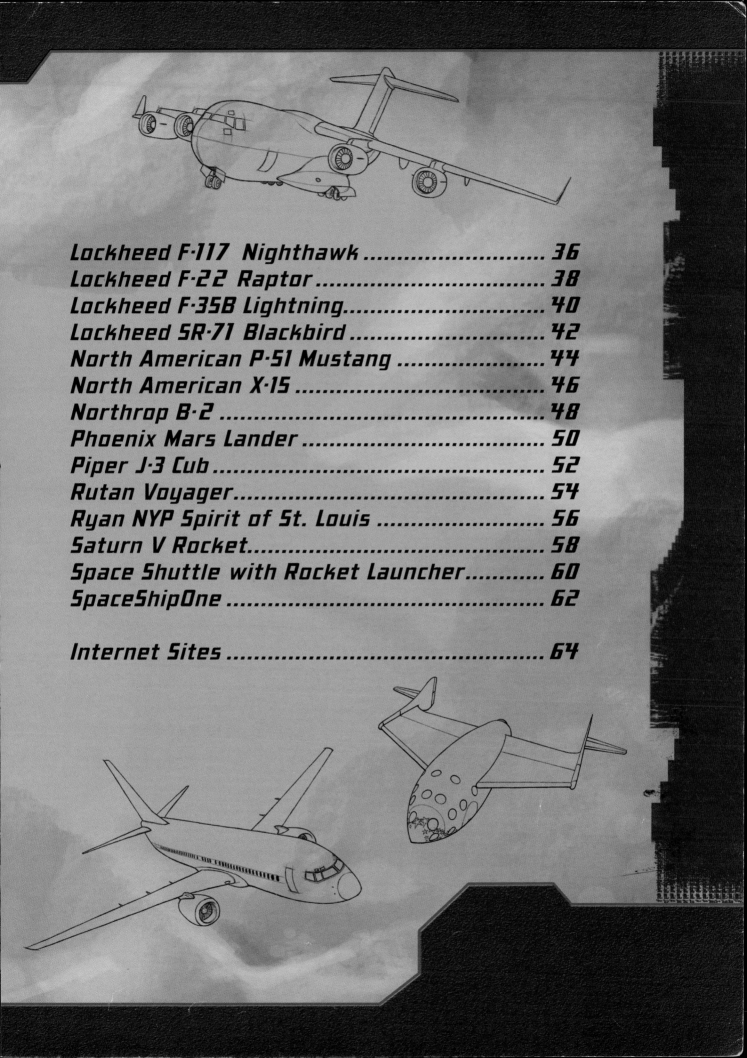

# 1903 WRIGHT FLYER

**STEP 1**

**STEP 2**

**STEP 3**

**STEP 4**

The Wright Flyer, built by brothers Orville and Wilbur Wright, was history's first heavier-than-air machine to fly successfully. Its first trip, piloted by Orville, was 121 feet (37 meters) long and lasted 12 seconds.

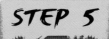

# APOLLO COMMAND MODULE

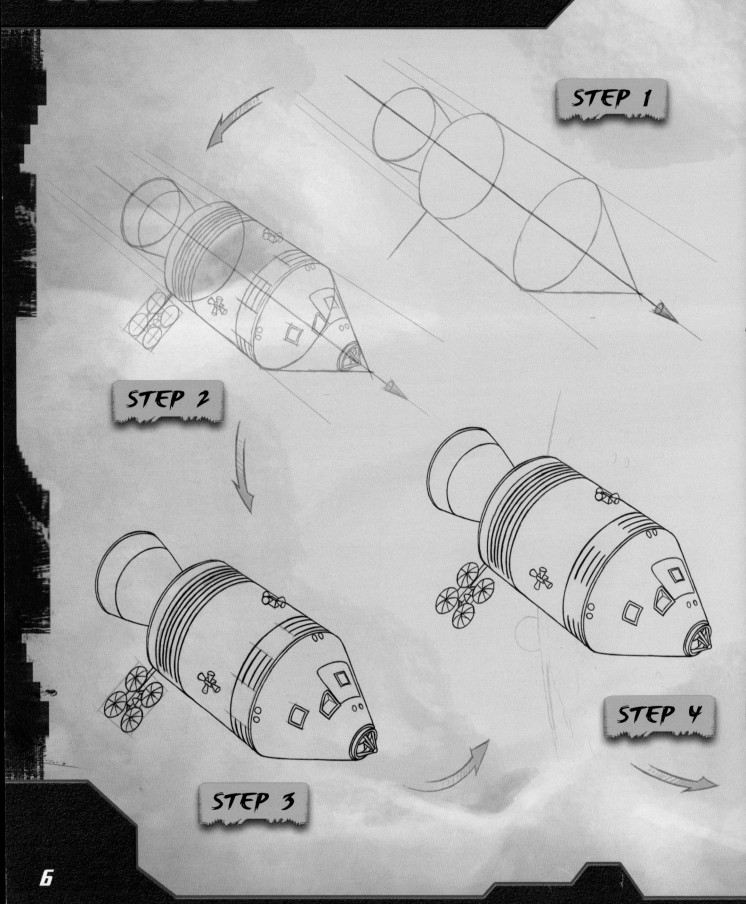

STEP 1

STEP 2

STEP 3

STEP 4

The Apollo command module *Columbia* completed the first manned lunar landing mission in 1969. It carried Neil Armstrong, Edwin "Buzz" Aldrin, and Michael Collins. The *Columbia* returned to Earth by splashing down in the Pacific Ocean.

FINISHED!

STEP 5

# ARLINGTON SISU 1A

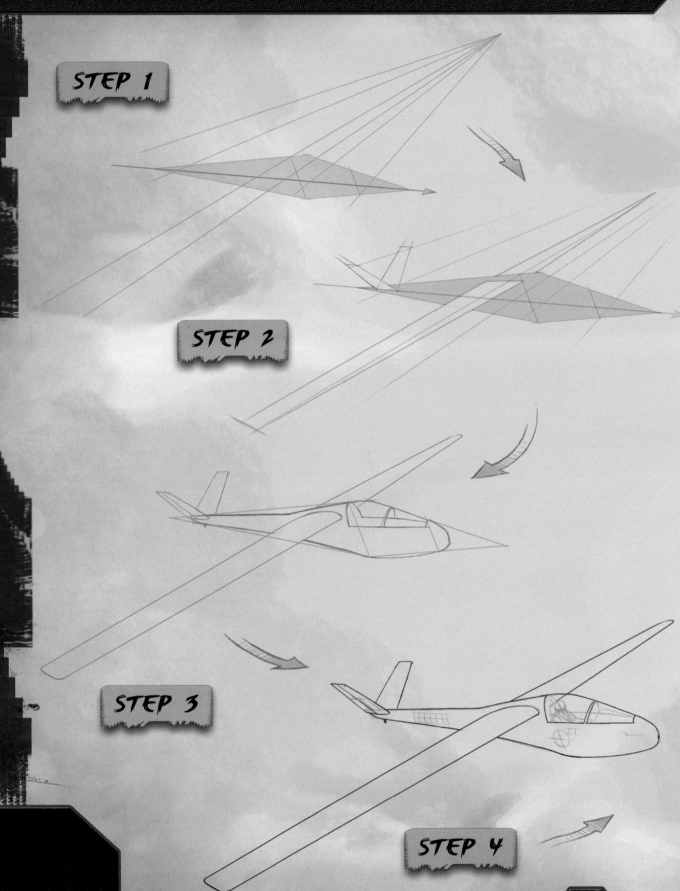

STEP 1

STEP 2

STEP 3

STEP 4

The *Sisu* is the most successful American competition sailplane (glider) ever flown. Extremely lightweight, this motorless aircraft was launched from a tow plane and was able to climb in rising air to gain altitude. In 1964 the *Sisu* soared a record 647 miles (1,040 kilometers).

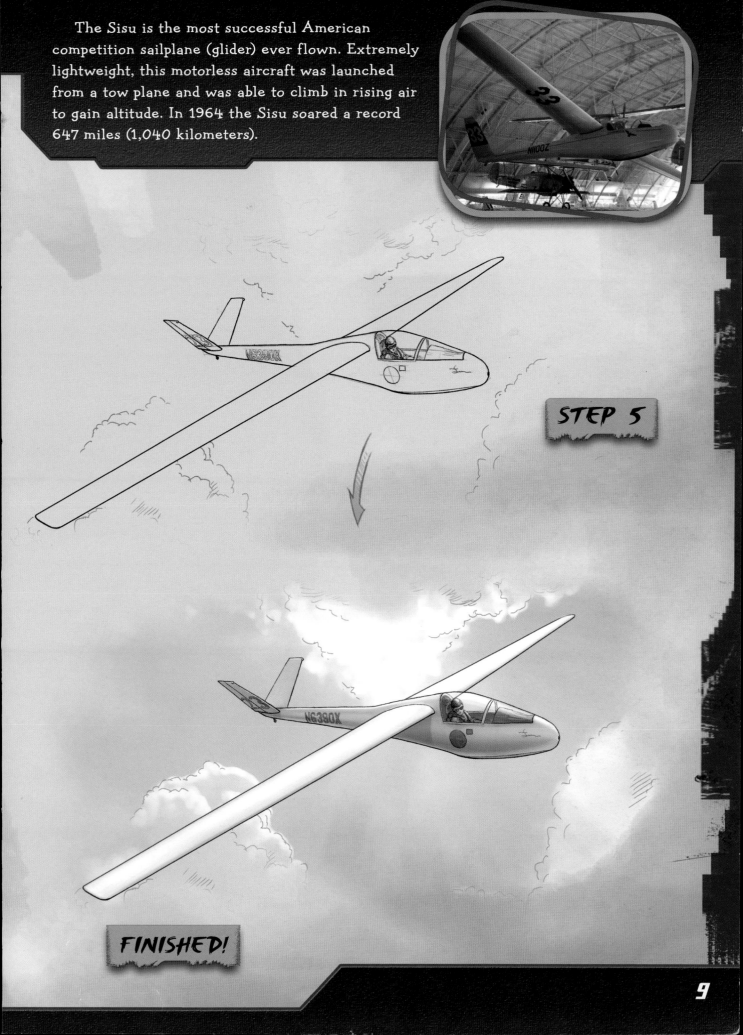

STEP 5

FINISHED!

# BELL AH-1 SUPER COBRA

STEP 1

STEP 2

STEP 3

STEP 4

Designed for the U.S. Marine Corps, this all-weather attack helicopter carries out a range of missions. Using Super Cobras in Operation Desert Shield/Desert Storm, the U.S. Marine Corps destroyed 97 tanks, 104 armored vehicles, and 16 bunkers without the loss of any aircraft.

STEP 5

FINISHED!

STEP 3

STEP 4

The rocket-engined Bell X-1 was the first aircraft to travel faster than the speed of sound—it reached Mach 1.06 in 1947. It also set altitude and other velocity records for a manned aircraft in later flights. It was typically launched from the bomb bay of a Boeing B-29.

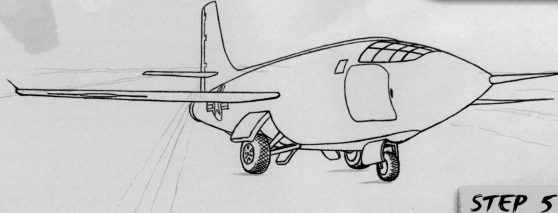

STEP 5

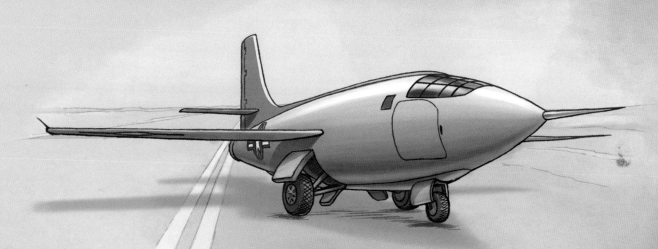

FINISHED!

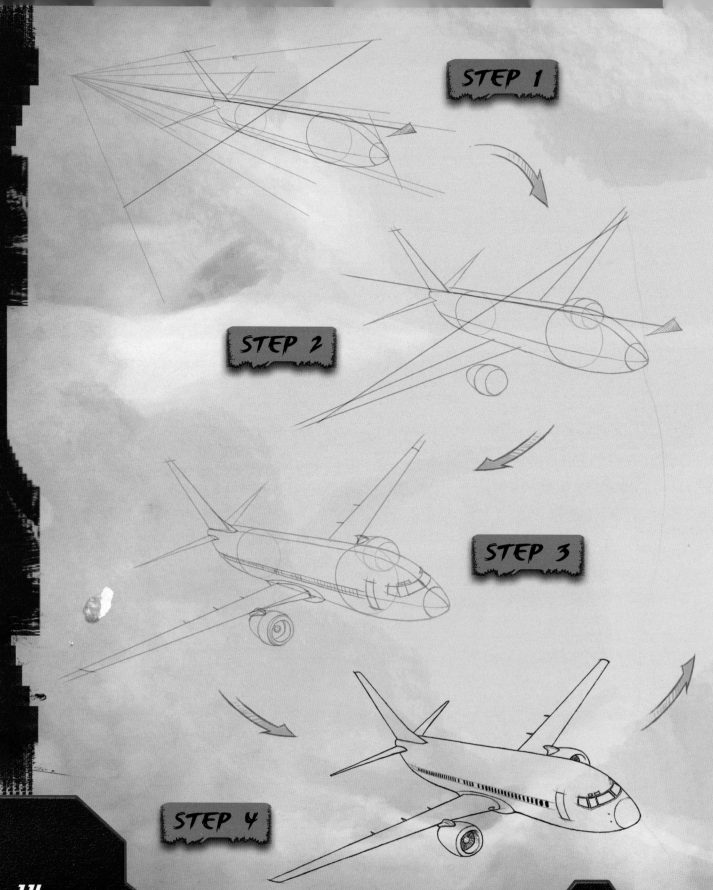

STEP 1

STEP 2

STEP 3

STEP 4

First flown in 1967, the 737 series is the best-selling line of passenger jets in history. There are so many of these jets in service that Boeing estimates there is a 737 taking off somewhere in the world every 5.3 seconds.

**STEP 5**

**FINISHED!**

# BOEING B-17 FLYING FORTRESS

STEP 1

STEP 2

STEP 3

STEP 4

The Boeing B-17 was the first four-engine long-range heavy bomber to serve with the U.S. Army Air Forces during World War II (1939–1945). It destroyed targets in Germany and Occupied Europe. More armor and weapons were added with each new version produced.

STEP 5

FINISHED!

# BOEING B-52 STRATOFORTRESS

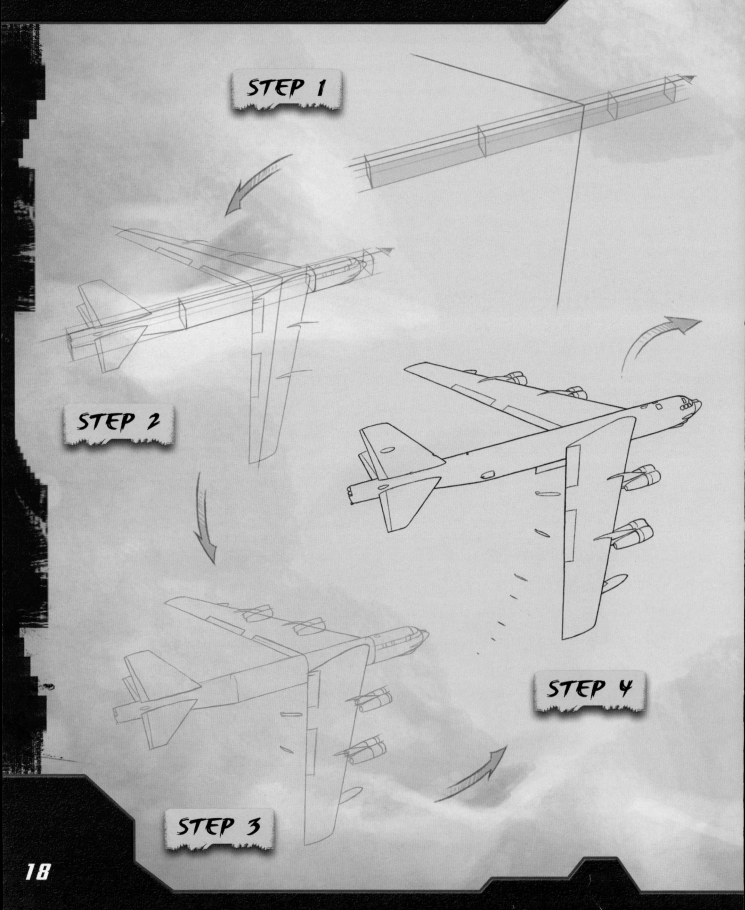

STEP 1

STEP 2

STEP 3

STEP 4

The B-52 is a long-range heavy bomber capable of dropping or launching the widest range of weapons in the U.S. military. This useful aircraft is still in service more than 50 years after it was introduced.

STEP 5

FINISHED!

# BOEING C-17 GLOBEMASTER

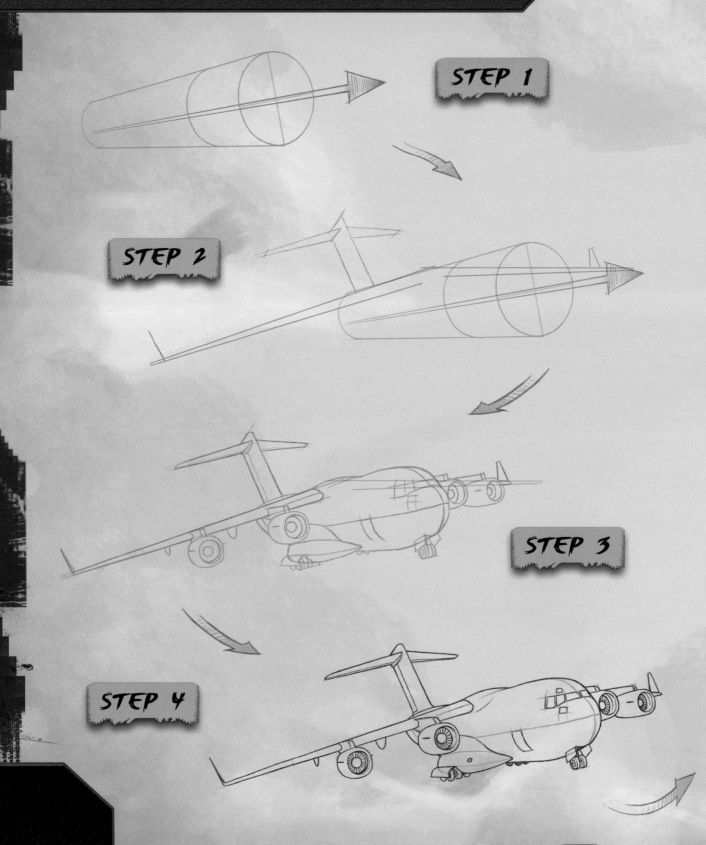

STEP 1

STEP 2

STEP 3

STEP 4

This massive military transport aircraft has delivered cargo in every worldwide operation since the 1990s. It can carry 160,000 pounds (73,000 kilograms) of cargo, which might include up to three Bradley infantry-fighting vehicles.

**STEP 5**

**FINISHED!**

# BOEING F-15 EAGLE

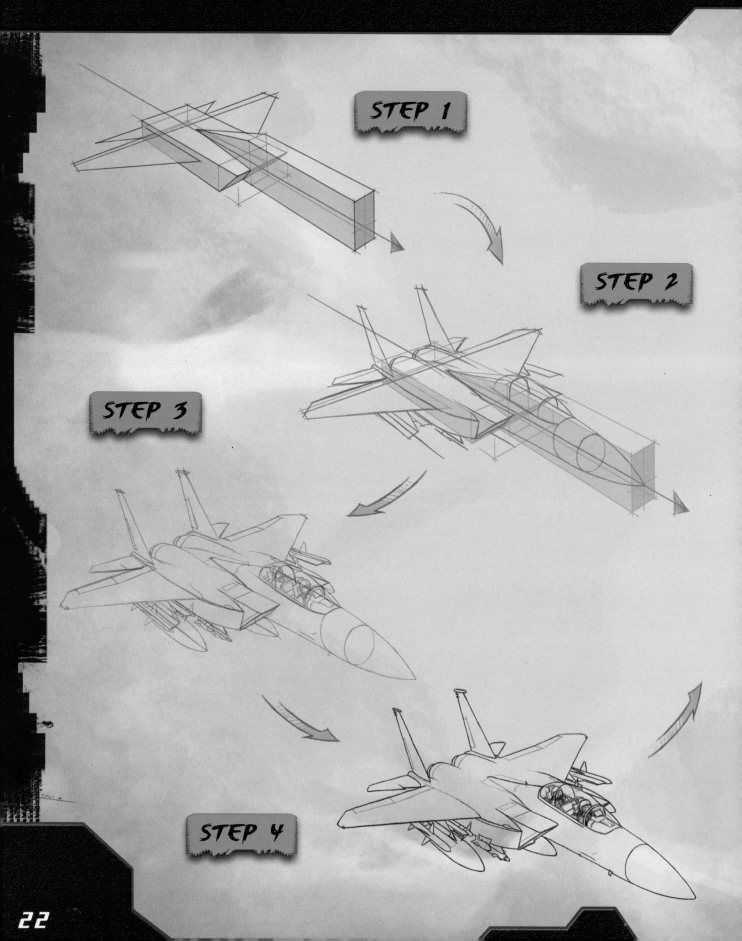

STEP 1

STEP 2

STEP 3

STEP 4

Noted for its exceptional power and maneuverability, the F-15 is an excellent fighter that features a unique "head-up" display. It shows all flight information on the windscreen so the pilot doesn't have to look down at the control panel.

STEP 5

FINISHED!

STEP 1

STEP 2

STEP 3

STEP 4

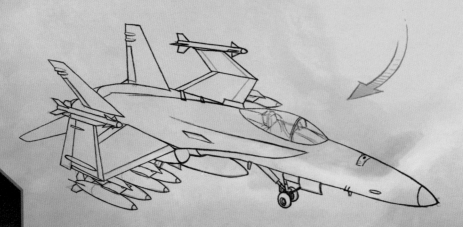

Designed to fly from aircraft carriers, the F/A-18 Hornet is a twin-engine multimission aircraft. It can switch from air-to-air fighter missions to air-to-ground strike missions with the flip of a switch. It has been deployed by the armed services of eight countries.

STEP 5

FINISHED!

# CONCORDE

STEP 1

STEP 2

STEP 3

STEP 4

This retired commercial passenger aircraft cruised at twice the speed of sound. The Concorde no longer makes its 3½-hour-transatlantic flights because operating costs were too high.

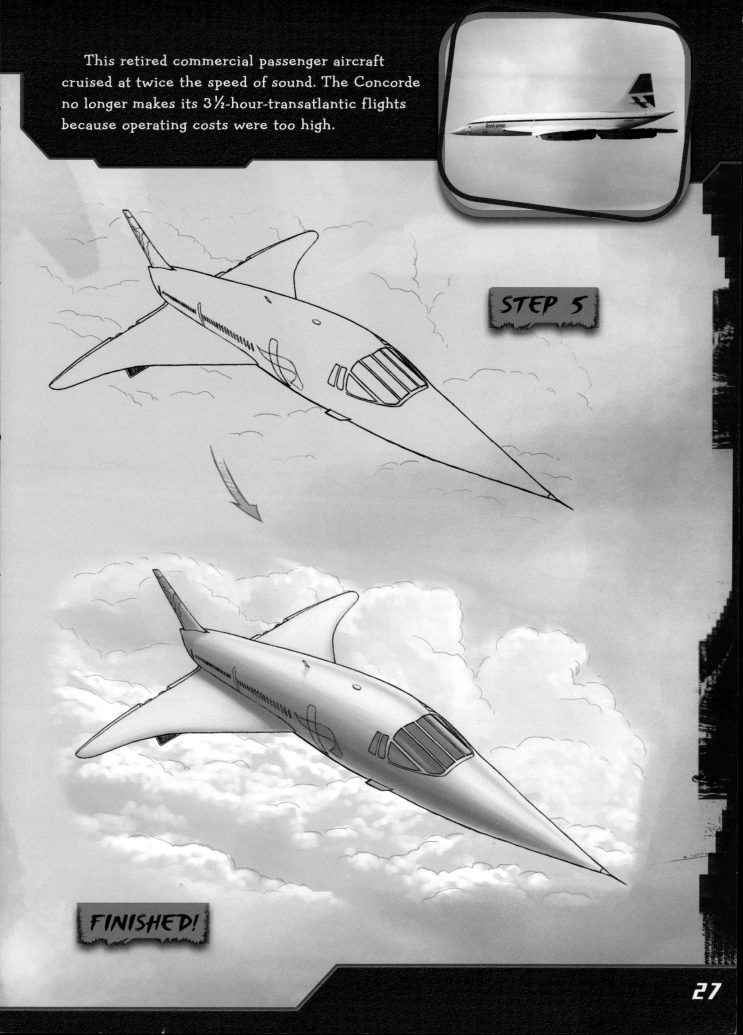

**STEP 5**

**FINISHED!**

# EXPLORER 1

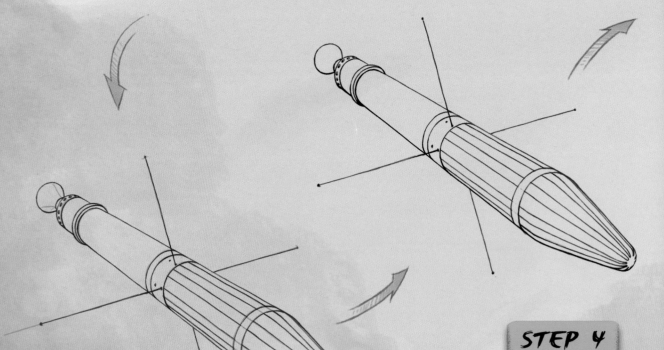

STEP 1

STEP 2

STEP 3

STEP 4

Considered America's first spacecraft, *Explorer 1* launched the United States into the Space Age in 1958. This satellite orbited Earth 58,000 times and re-entered Earth's atmosphere in 1970, after 12 years in space. It weighed only about 31 pounds (14 kilograms).

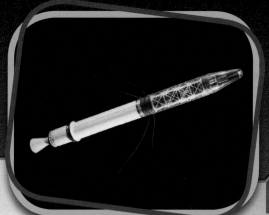

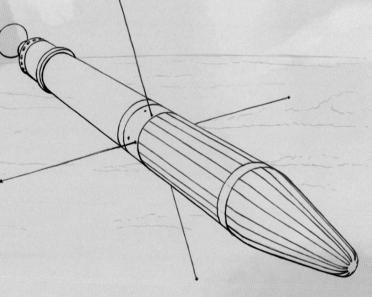

STEP 5

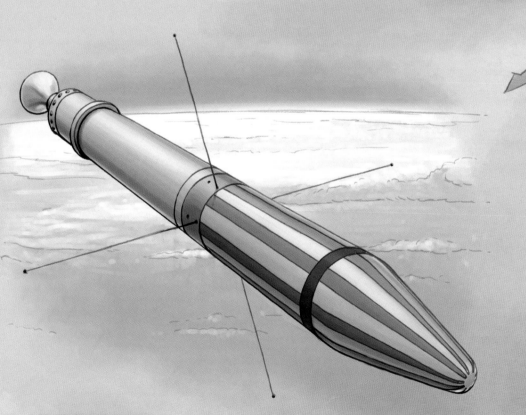

FINISHED!

# GENERAL ATOMICS MQ-1 PREDATOR

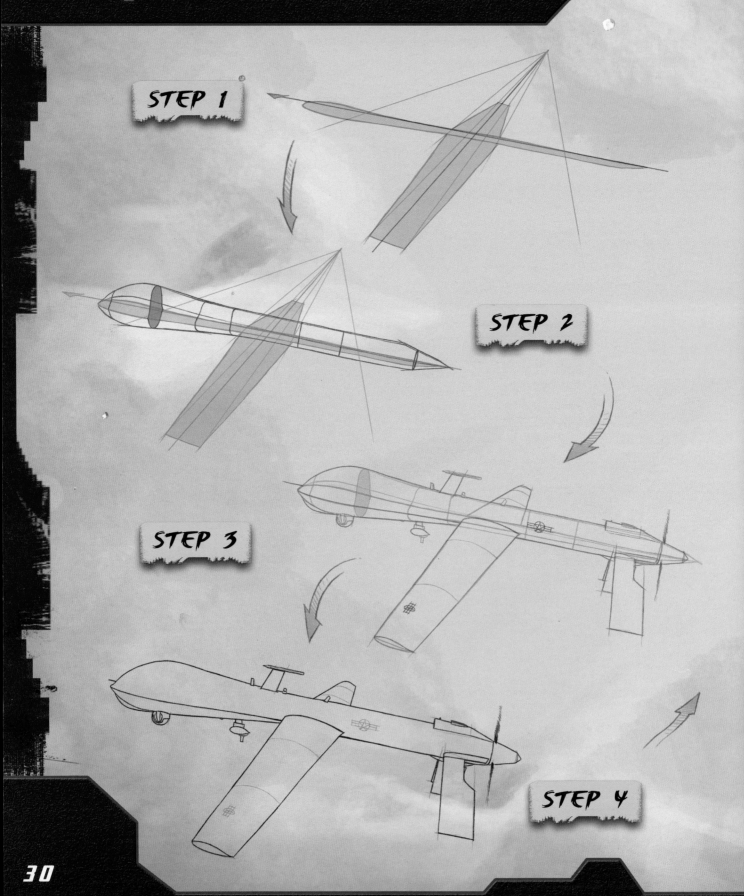

STEP 1

STEP 2

STEP 3

STEP 4

The Predator unmanned aerial vehicle is a complex reconnaissance and attack system operated from a ground control station. The Predator gathers information and has munitions capabilities—it can deploy two laser-guided, highly accurate Hellfire missiles.

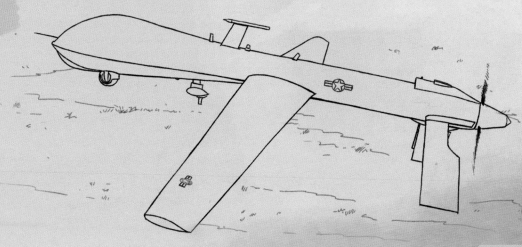

**STEP 5**

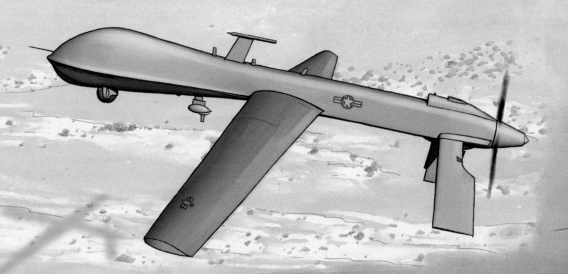

**FINISHED!**

# GRUMMAN EA-6B PROWLER

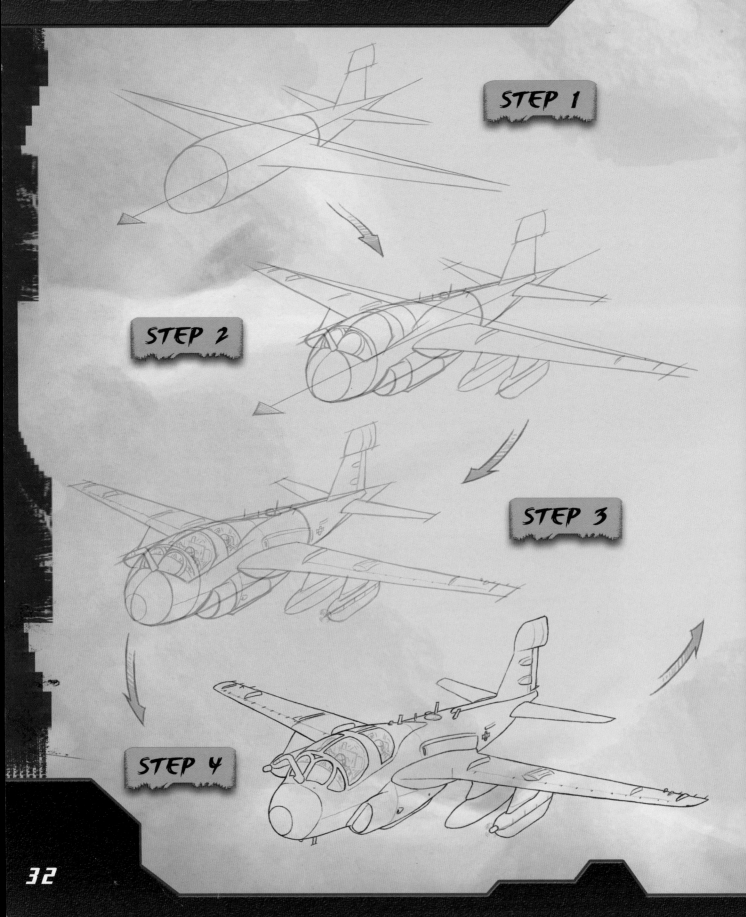

STEP 1

STEP 2

STEP 3

STEP 4

The EA-6B Prowler was designed to attack enemy electronic communication by jamming its radar. This protects strike aircraft and ground troops. The Prowler is also able to pick up signals from enemy communications.

STEP 5

FINISHED!

# GRUMMAN F-14 TOMCAT

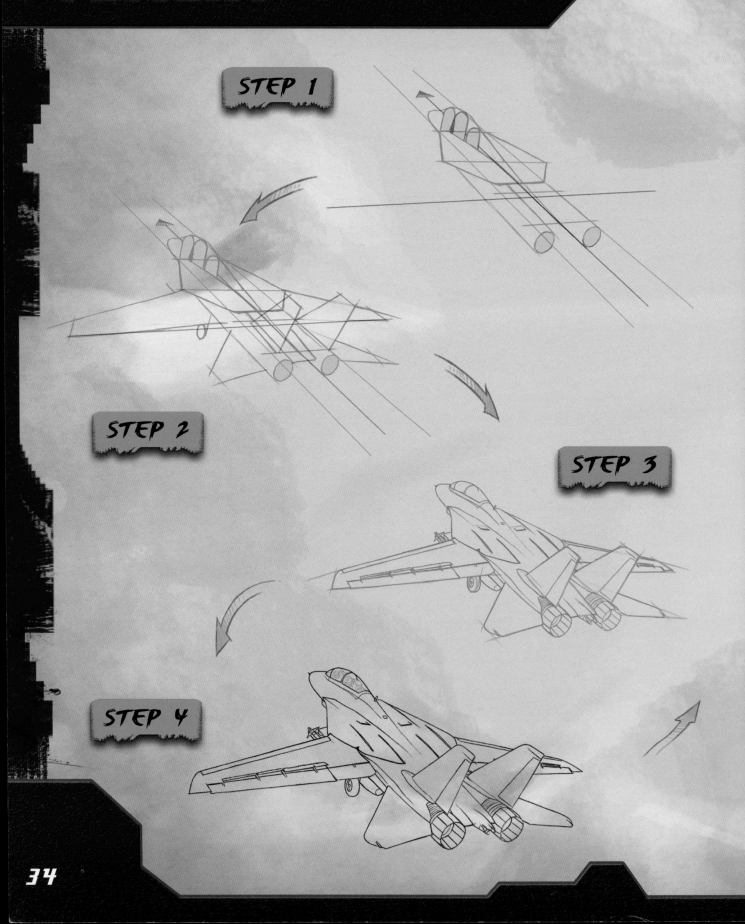

STEP 1

STEP 2

STEP 3

STEP 4

The F-14 Tomcat is a supersonic twin-engine strike fighter. The pilot and the radar intercept officer work together to navigate, find targets, and deploy weapons. They also conduct electronic countermeasures, which trick the enemy's detection systems.

STEP 5

FINISHED!

# LOCKHEED F-117 NIGHTHAWK

STEP 1

STEP 2

STEP 3

STEP 4

This first "stealth" fighter was developed in total secrecy. It was first flown in 1981, but it was not publicly announced until 1988. The Nighthawk was made for nighttime attack missions and proved successful during both Gulf wars.

STEP 5

FINISHED!

# LOCKHEED F-22 RAPTOR

STEP 1

STEP 2

STEP 3

STEP 4

This new stealth fighter is able to track, identify, shoot, and kill air-to-air threats, all before even being detected. The F-22 is a multimission fighter, designed for intelligence gathering, surveillance, reconnaissance, and electronic attacks.

STEP 5

FINISHED!

# LOCKHEED F-35B LIGHTNING

STEP 1

STEP 2

STEP 4

STEP 3

The F-35B is designed with short takeoff/vertical landing (STOVL) capabilities. This gives the stealth fighter and attack aircraft the unique ability to take off from small ships, roads, or undeveloped areas.

**STEP 5**

**FINISHED!**

# LOCKHEED SR-71 BLACKBIRD

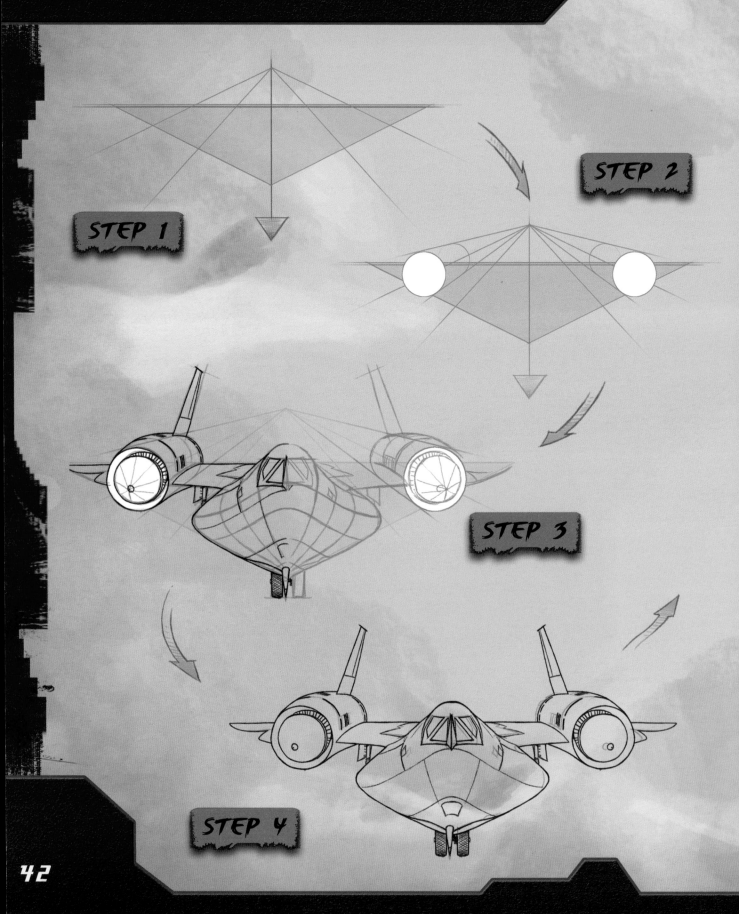

STEP 1

STEP 2

STEP 3

STEP 4

First flown in the 1960s, the SR-71 is the world's fastest jet-powered aircraft, capable of flying faster than Mach 3.2. Built as a reconnaissance aircraft, its missions were to photograph high value targets from an altitude of 80,000 feet (24,380 meters).

**STEP 5**

**FINISHED!**

# NORTH AMERICAN P-51 MUSTANG

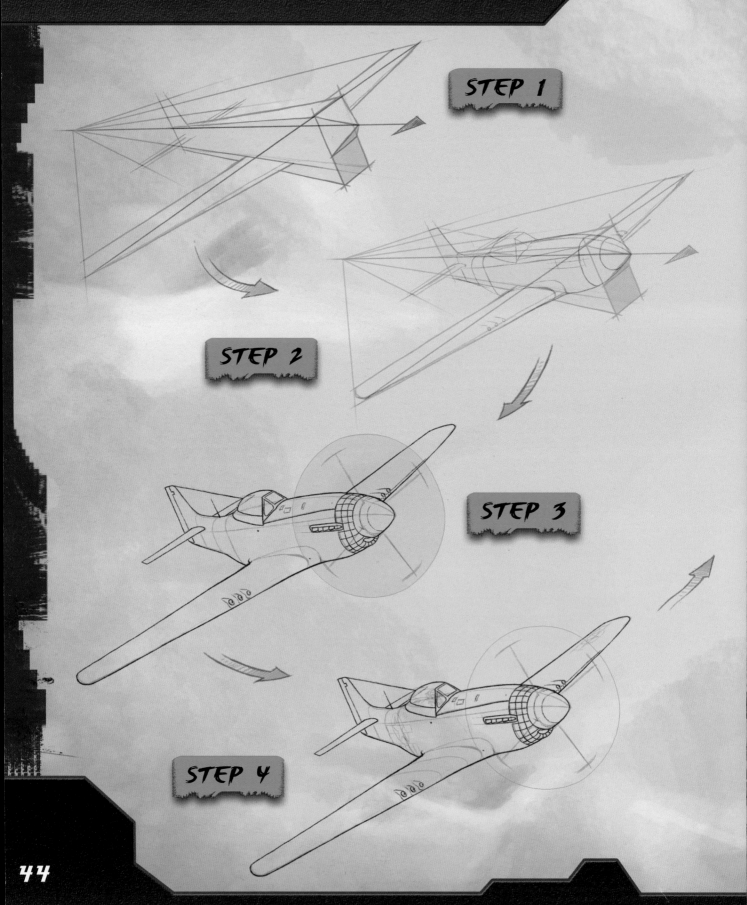

STEP 1

STEP 2

STEP 3

STEP 4

The P-51 Mustang was the best-performing long-range escort fighter of World War II. It was capable of great speed and high-altitude performance.

**STEP 5**

**FINISHED!**

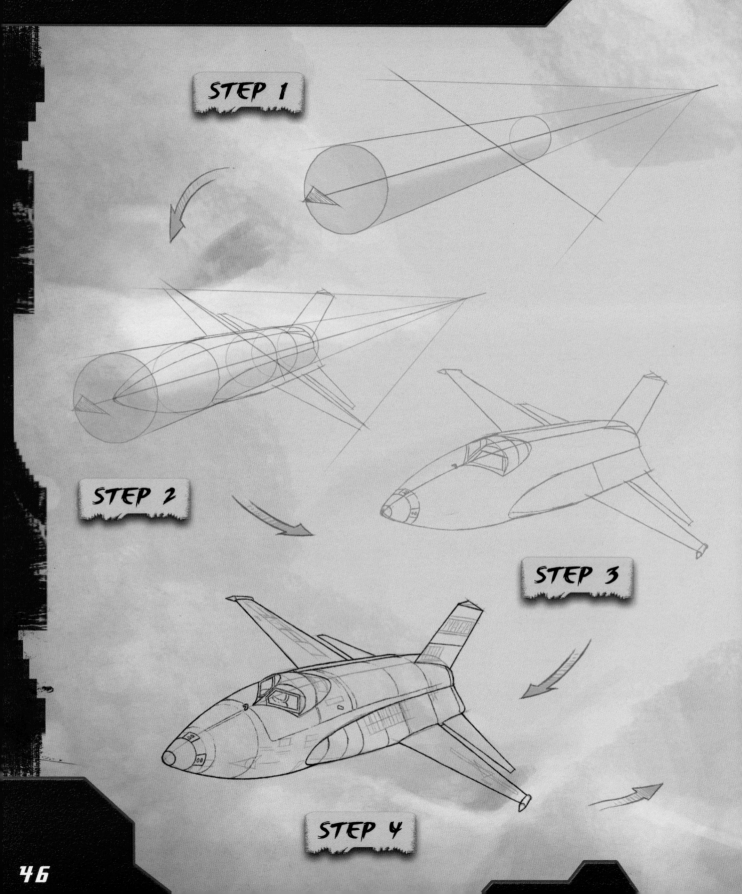

STEP 1

STEP 2

STEP 3

STEP 4

This rocket-powered research aircraft was the first winged craft to reach Mach 4, 5, and 6—four, five, and six times the speed of sound—during 199 test flights between 1959 and 1967.

STEP 5

FINISHED!

# NORTHROP B-2

STEP 1

STEP 2

STEP 3

STEP 4

The B-2 is an American heavy bomber with a flying wing design. Its technology allows it to fly undetected by many defense systems. It can carry up to 40,000 pounds (18,000 kilograms) of weapons, including nuclear weapons.

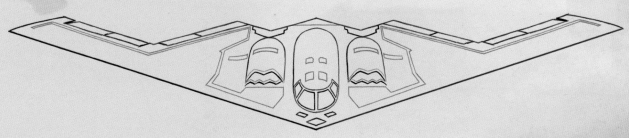

STEP 5

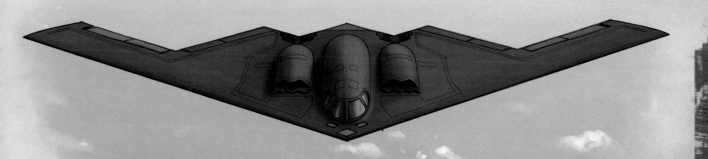

**FINISHED!**

# PHOENIX MARS LANDER

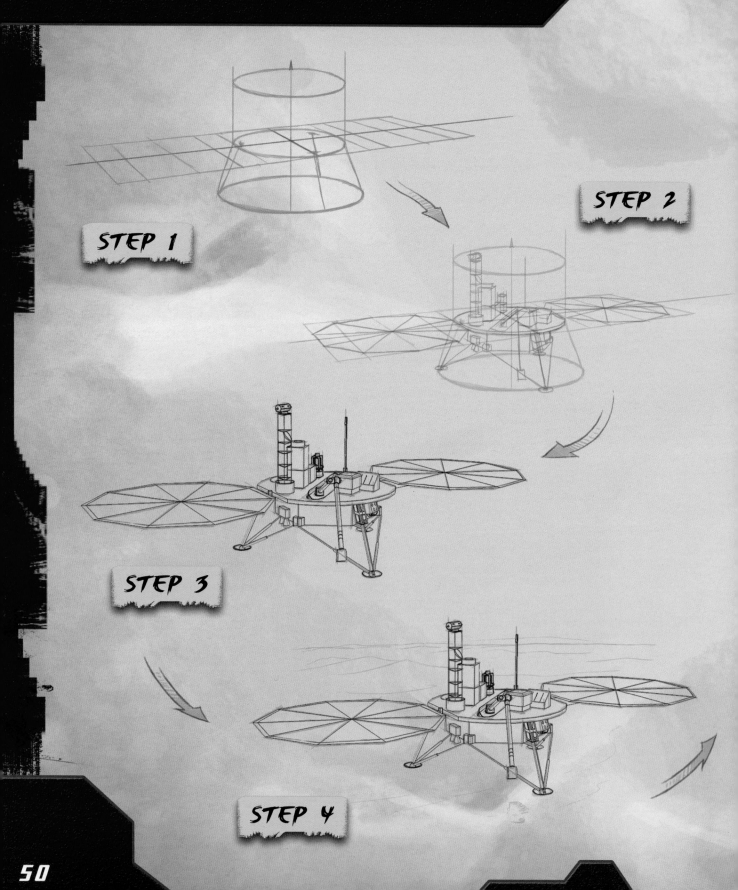

STEP 1

STEP 2

STEP 3

STEP 4

This robotic spacecraft landed on Mars in 2008 to conduct research. It was launched with a Delta rocket and used solar power while on Mars.

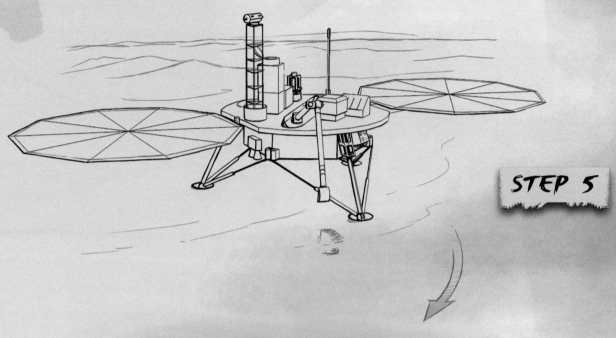

STEP 5

FINISHED!

# PIPER J-3 CUB

STEP 1

STEP 2

STEP 3

STEP 4

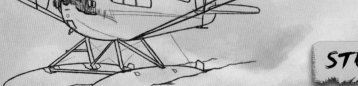

Thousands of pilots learned to fly in a Piper J-3 Cub during the 1930s and 1940s. By the end of World War II, 80 percent of all U.S. military pilots had received flight training in these small yellow planes. Some have "floats" on the bottom for water landings.

STEP 5

FINISHED!

# RUTAN VOYAGER

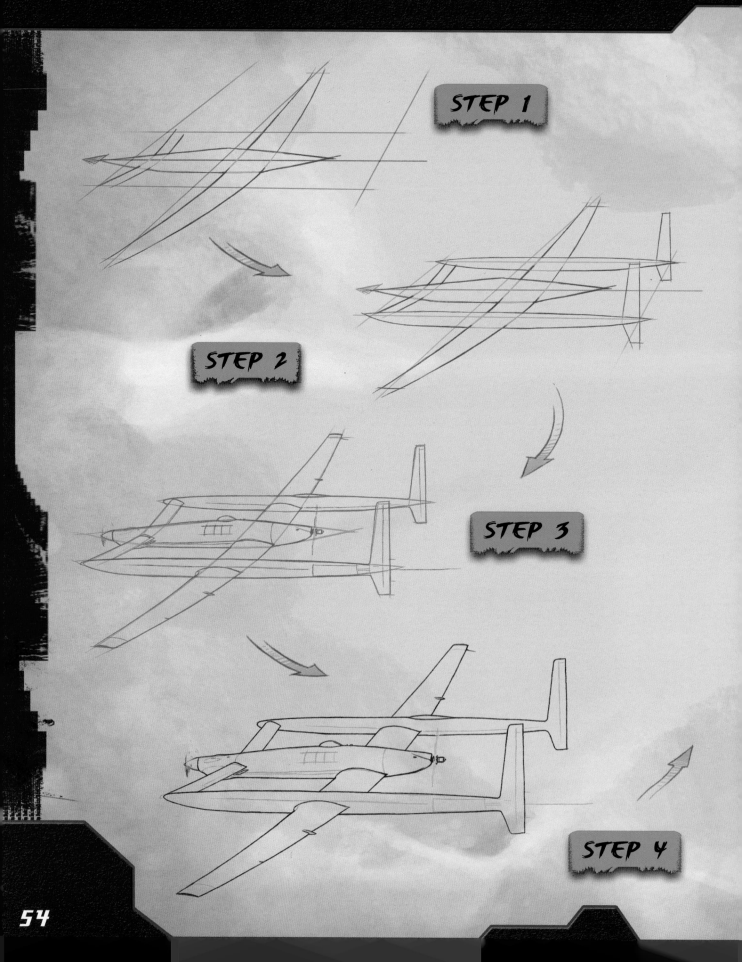

STEP 1

STEP 2

STEP 3

STEP 4

The airframe of this extremely lightweight aircraft is made without metal. The main wing is so flexible that it can bend up to 5 feet (1.5 meters) while in flight. Considered a "flying fuel tank," the Voyager completed the first nonstop, nonrefueled flight around the world in 1986.

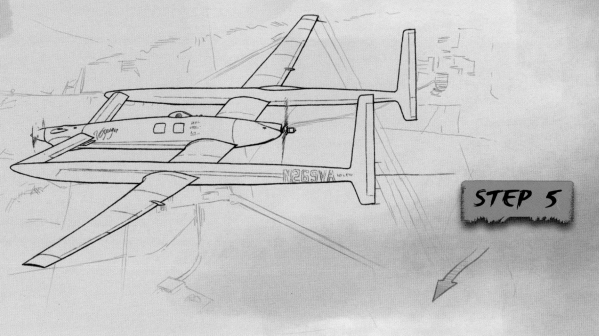

STEP 5

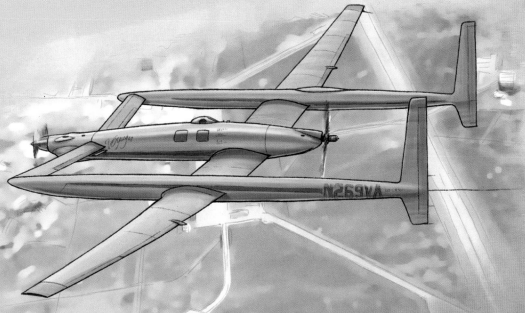

FINISHED!

# RYAN NYP SPIRIT OF ST. LOUIS

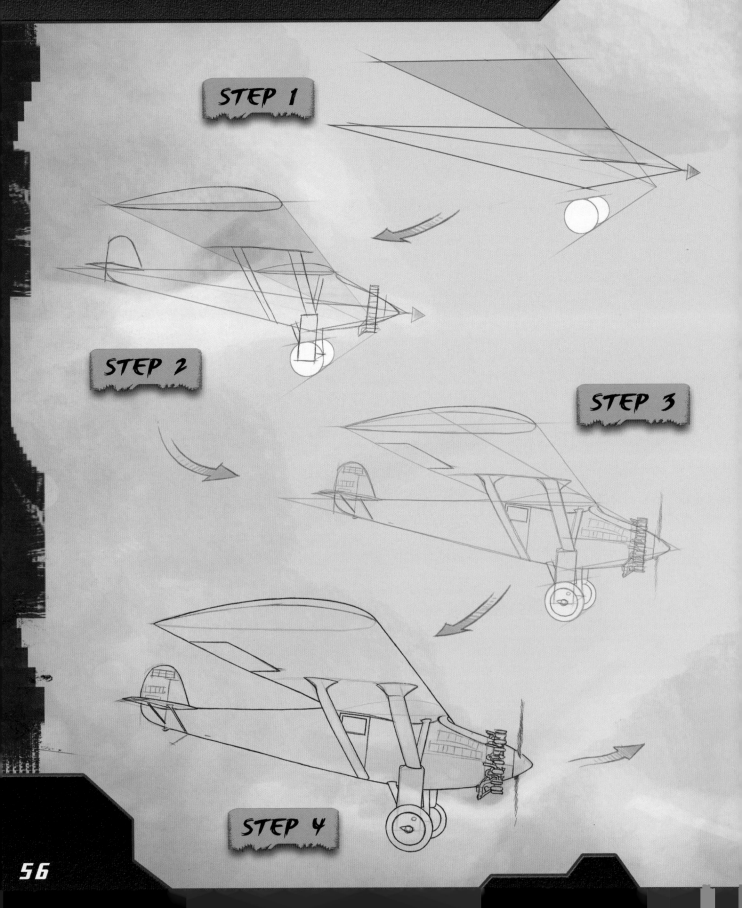

STEP 1

STEP 2

STEP 3

STEP 4

In 1927 the *Spirit of St. Louis*, flown by Charles A. Lindbergh, completed the first solo nonstop transatlantic flight in history. It flew from New York to Paris, which is what the NYP stands for, in 33 hours and 30 minutes.

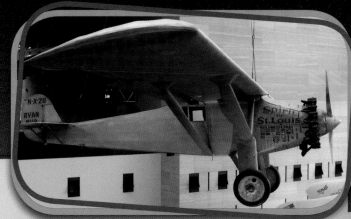

STEP 5

FINISHED!

# SATURN V ROCKET

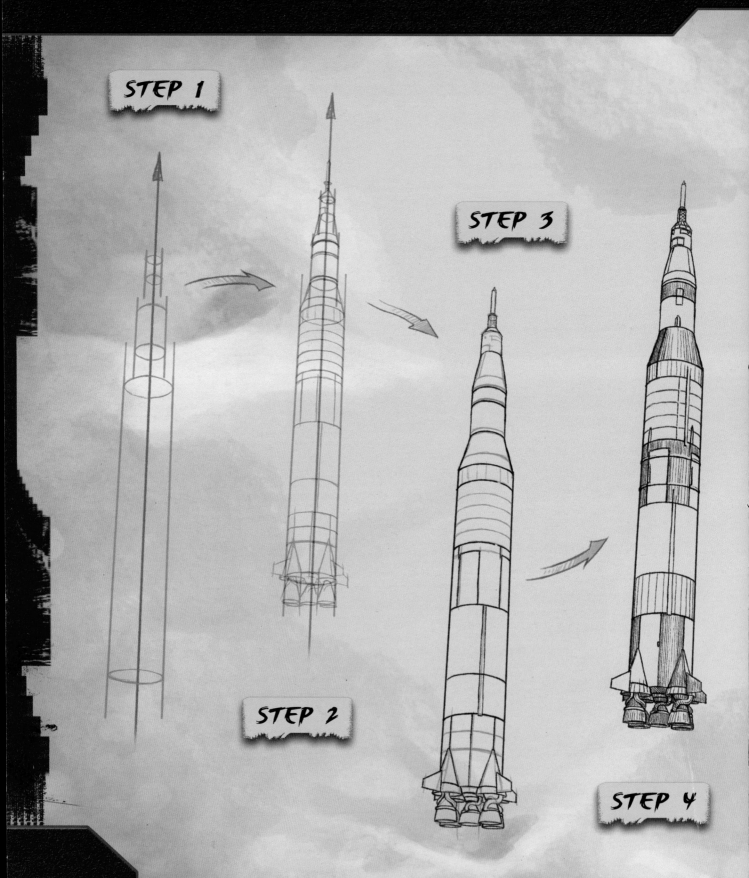

STEP 1

STEP 2

STEP 3

STEP 4

Saturn V was a liquid-propellant rocket that was taller than the Statue of Liberty. The first manned Saturn V mission sent the Apollo 8 astronauts into orbit around the moon in December 1968.

STEP 5

FINISHED!

# SPACE SHUTTLE WITH ROCKET LAUNCHER

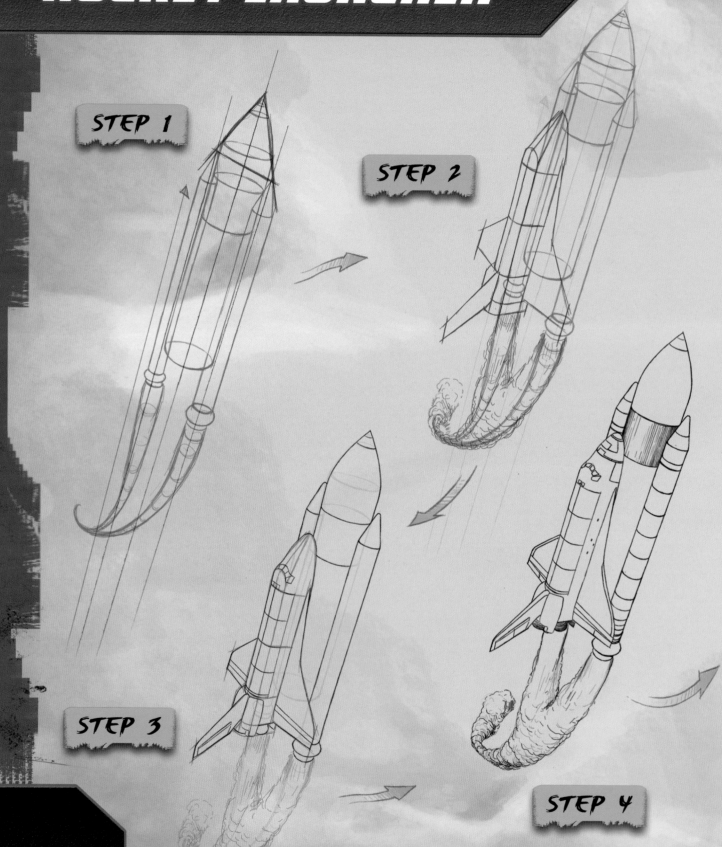

STEP 1

STEP 2

STEP 3

STEP 4

Beginning in 1981 the space shuttle program ran for 30 years, flying 135 missions. The shuttle was the world's first reusable spacecraft, and there were five in the fleet. Including its twin solid rocket boosters, the vehicle system consisted of about 2.5 million moving parts.

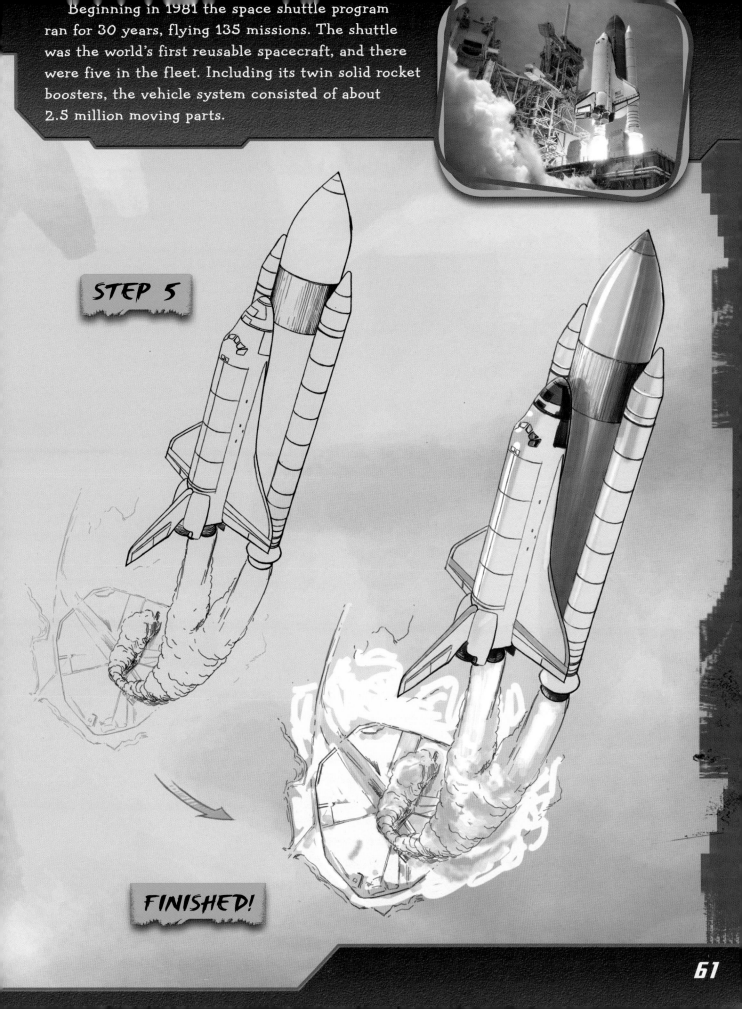

STEP 5

FINISHED!

STEP 1

STEP 2

STEP 3

STEP 4

SpaceShipOne is the first privately developed piloted vehicle to reach space. This rocket-powered aircraft can change shape to provide a safe and smooth return from space into Earth's atmosphere. The goal of SpaceShipOne is to give people a chance to get to space affordably.

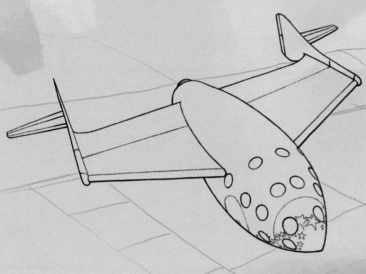

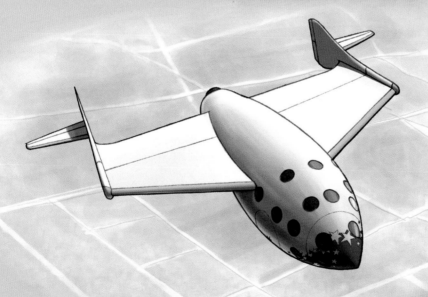

Capstone Press
1710 Roe Crest Drive
North Mankato, Minnesota 56003
www.capstonepub.com

Library of Congress Cataloging-in-Publication Data
How to draw amazing airplanes and spacecraft / by Kristen
McCurry ; illustrated by Mat Edwards.
pages c.m. — (Smithsonian drawing books)
Summary: "Provides information and step-by-step drawing
instructions for 30 air and space craft"—Provided by
publisher.
  ISBN 978-1-4296-8749-2 (library binding)
  ISBN 978-1-4296-9448-3 (paperback)
1. Airplanes in art—Juvenile literature. 2. Space ships in
art—Juvenile literature. 3. Drawing—Technique—Juvenile
literature. I. Edwards, Mat, 1966- illustrator. II. Title.
  NC825.A4M38 2013
  743'.8962912—dc23                    2012002885

**Editorial Credits:**
Kristen Mohn, editor
Alison Thiele, designer
Nathan Gassman, art director
Deirdre Barton and Eric Gohl, media researchers
Kathy McColley, production specialist

Our very special thanks to F. Robert van der Linden,
chairman of the Aeronautics Division at the National Air
and Space Museum & Paul E. Ceruzzi, chairman of the Space
History Division at the National Air and Space Museum
for their curatorial review. Capstone would also like to
thank Ellen Nanney and Kealy Wilson at the Smithsonian
Institution's Office of Licensing for their help in the
creation of this book.

Smithsonian Enterprises: Carol LeBlanc, Vice President;
Brigid Ferraro, Director of Licensing

**Photo/Illustration credits:**
BAE Systems: 27; Boeing Management Company: 15, 17, 19,
21, 23, 25, 39, 45, 47, 59; Mojave Aerospace Ventures, LLC:
63; Northrop Grumman Systems Corporation: 33, 35, 49;
Wikipedia: Ad Meskens, 57, Arpingstone, 53, Cliff, 9, NASA,
7, 13, 29, 51, 55, 61, Public Domain, 5, U.S. Air Force, 31, 37,
43, U.S. Marine Corps, 11, U.S. Navy, 41

Every effort has been made to contact copyright
holders of material reproduced in this book.
Any omissions will be rectified in subsequent
printings if notice is given to the publishers.

# INTERNET SITES

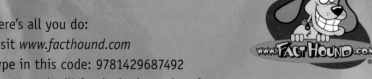

FactHound offers a safe, fun way to find Internet sites
related to this book. All of the sites on FactHound have
been researched by our staff.

Here's all you do:
Visit *www.facthound.com*
Type in this code: 9781429687492
FactHound will fetch the best sites for you!

Check out projects, games and lots more at
www.capstonekids.com

Printed in the United States of America in North Mankato, Minnesota.
042012    006682CGF12